Contents

Getting started

3. Using my journal............................☐
4. Our Essential Agreements ....☐
6. Reflecting on my learner profile......☐
9. Taking action ....☐

Self-management skills

10. Setting goals ....☐
11. Planning achievable goals ....☐
12. Persevering to achieve goals ....☐
13. Taking action ....☐
14. Emotions in conflict......................☐
15. Managing my emotions ....☐
16. Finding solutions to conflicts..........☐
17. Using strategies to resolve
      conflict ....☐
18. Mindfulness..................................☐
19. Overcoming distractions.................☐
20. Practising being present................☐
21. Using the senses ....☐
22. Taking action...............................☐
23. Self-motivation ....☐
24. Using positive thinking...................☐
25. Reflecting on my mindset ....☐
26. Taking action...............................☐

Social skills

27. Interpersonal relationships............☐
28. Collaboration ....☐
29. Teamwork....................................☐
30. Taking action...............................☐

Communication skills

31. Exchanging information ....☐
32. Listening to others speak...............☐
33. Speaking to an audience ....☐
34. Asking for help and support...........☐
35. Giving and receiving feedback........☐
36. Taking action...............................☐
37. Ways of communicating ....☐
38. Trying different types of
      communication.............................☐
39. Planning how to communicate........☐
40. Taking action...............................☐

Thinking skills

41. Transferring knowledge...................☐

43. My metacognition..........................☐

44. Making connections.......................☐

45. Using metacognition to help
    my learning ....☐

46. Critical and creative thinking ....☐

47. Thinking critically ....☐

48. Applying creative thinking ....☐

50. Thinking and planning action ....☐

52. Transferring knowledge:
    the SDGs ....☐

55. What is taking action?...................☐

56. Reflecting on action.....................☐

58. How might the learner profile
    connect with change?....................☐

Research skills

60. Sources of information ....☐

62. Forming questions ....☐

63. Using my thinking skills to
    develop an inquiry..........................☐

64. Reflecting on my inquiry ....☐

66. Using media ethically....................☐

67. Finding trusted sources of
    information ....☐

68. Using the internet responsibly.......☐

69. Taking action ....☐

Final reflections

70. Reflecting on my year....................☐

72. What's next? ....☐

Welcome

This is your journal. Please use it to draw or write your ideas and thoughts.

There are no right or wrong answers – be free to explore.

Reflection helps us to develop an awareness of ourselves and others.

Reflection can be …

Being aware of the present. Describing your feelings.

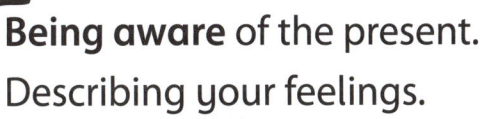

Wondering.
Giving your point of view.
Making connections.

Thinking back on your day. Thinking forward about how to improve.

Planning goals for yourself and next steps. Planning how to use your skills to take action.

Our Essential Agreements

Essential agreements help us to create the right learning environment.
Agreements that work for everyone = a great year!

How do you like to learn?

What makes you feel safe and supported at school?

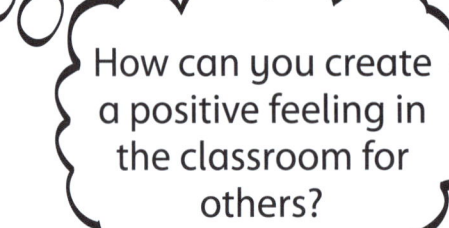

How can you create a positive feeling in the classroom for others?

How can you make sure everyone feels respected?

What would you like to see in your essential agreements?

 How do your ideas compare to others?

Reflecting on my learner profile

Being **reflective** about your learner profile helps you to understand yourself. Knowing this also helps you to understand others and be **caring**.

What do you see?

....

....

....

....

....

....

Tick four attributes to describe this boy. You can add your own ideas in the box.

 Balanced ☐

 Caring ☐

 Communicator ☐

 Inquirer ☐

 Knowledgeable ☐

 Open-minded ☐

 Principled ☐

 Reflective ☐

 Risk-taker ☐

 Thinker ☐

 Share your choices with a partner.

What do you notice?

Why might your answers be similar or different?

How would you assess your learner profile?
Add each attribute to a shape. The bigger the shape the more you show that attribute.

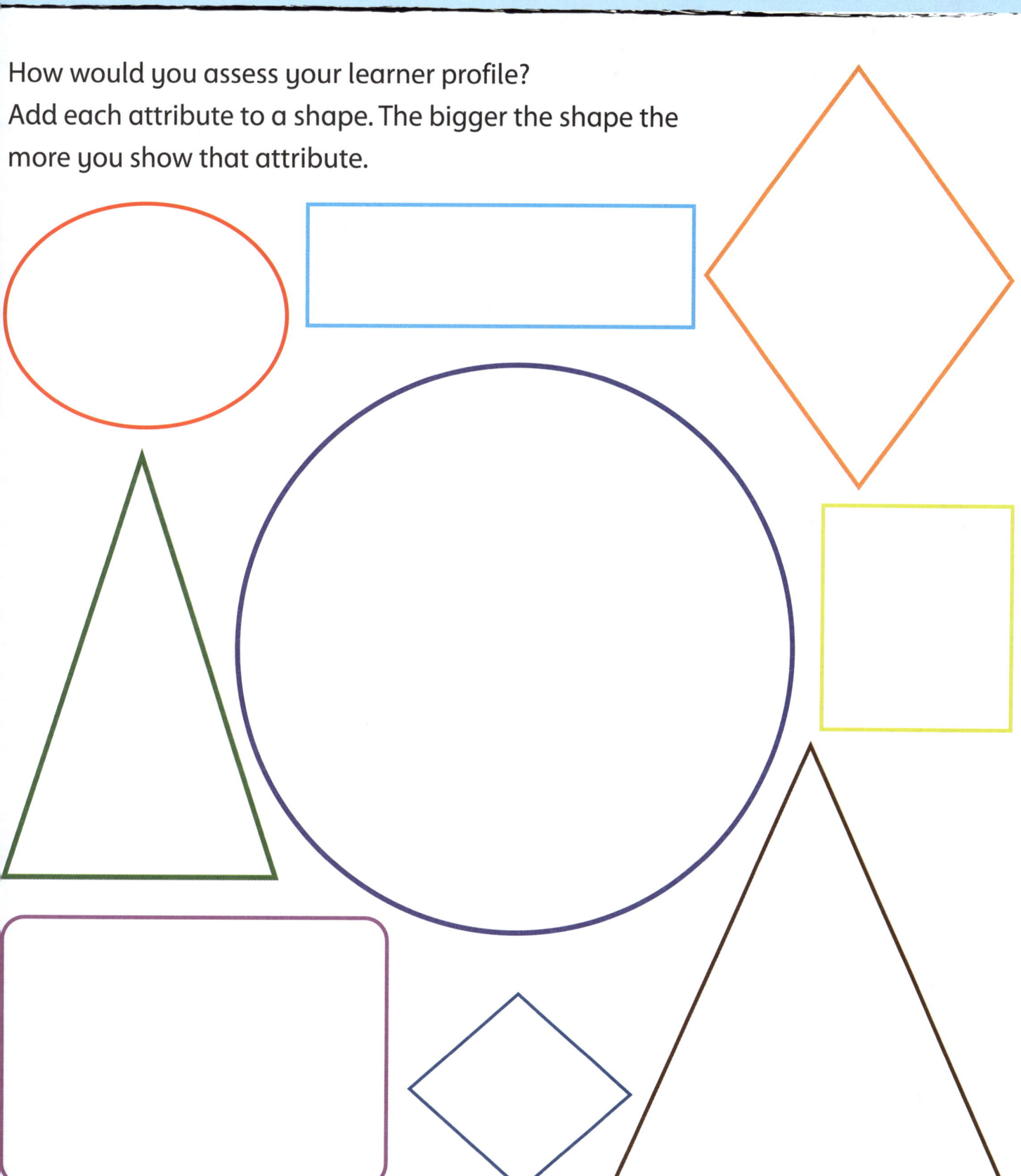

Talk to your partner about the attributes you show the most.
Which attributes can you develop?

Reflecting on my learner profile

When have you shown the learner profile attributes? Share some examples.

Taking action

☐ Think about your strengths.

☐ How could you use your strengths to help yourself or others?

☐ How could you use your learner profile attributes to take action?

Setting goals

Setting goals helps us be **reflective** and become **knowledgeable**. It also helps us organize our time and manage ourselves.

Think of three goals for this week.

A personal goal:

A friendship goal:

A school goal:

 How might being a **risk-taker** help you achieve your goals?

Planning achievable goals

☐ Choose one of your goals.

☐ Make an action plan. What steps will you take? What help and resources do you need?

☐ Break your goal into three small actions.

1

2

3

How will you know when you have reached your goal?

I will know I have reached my goal when ....

Persevering to achieve goals

We often face obstacles that can make it harder for us to achieve our goals. By showing perseverance and keeping going, we can achieve our goals.

Who and what can help me achieve my learning goals?

What are some obstacles that might get in the way?

What can I tell myself when it gets difficult?

 Which attributes do you use to set goals and work towards them?

 Balanced

 Communicator

 Knowledgeable

 Principled

 Risk-taker

 Caring

 Inquirer

 Open-minded

 Reflective

 Thinker

Taking action

1 Reflect on your goals. Use the checklist below.

- ☐ I have set short-term goals.
- ☐ I have planned my steps for taking action.
- ☐ I have managed obstacles.
- ☐ I have shown perseverance.

2 Choose one of your goals. How close are you to achieving it?
Mark where you are on the line.

I haven't achieved my goal yet.   Yes! I have achieved my goal.

What should you do next to get closer to achieving your goal?

....

....

....

....

....

....

....

....

Emotions in conflict

Conflict is a disagreement or a problem between people. If we are **open-minded** and **caring**, we can try to understand both sides of the situation.

Share a time when you experienced conflict.

Circle the face that shows how it made you feel. Then write about your feelings.

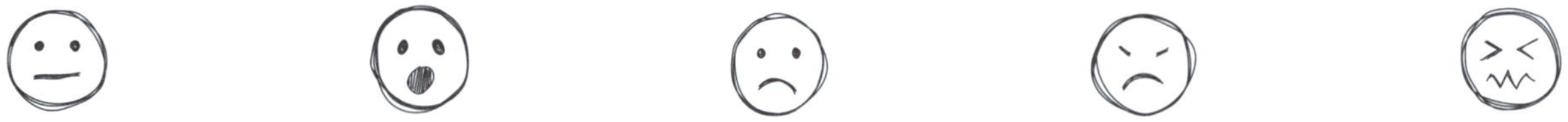

Managing my emotions

There are many ways we can manage our emotions. Sometimes, we have to try a few different ways before we find one that works for us.

Think about some things that upset you. What can you do to calm down?

☹ Things that upset me	☺ Ways I can calm down

Finding solutions to conflicts

Reflect on the Wheel of Choice.

- ☐ What might you add to this wheel? Fill in the blank spaces.
- ☐ What do you notice?
- ☐ Which of these solutions might NOT work well for you?

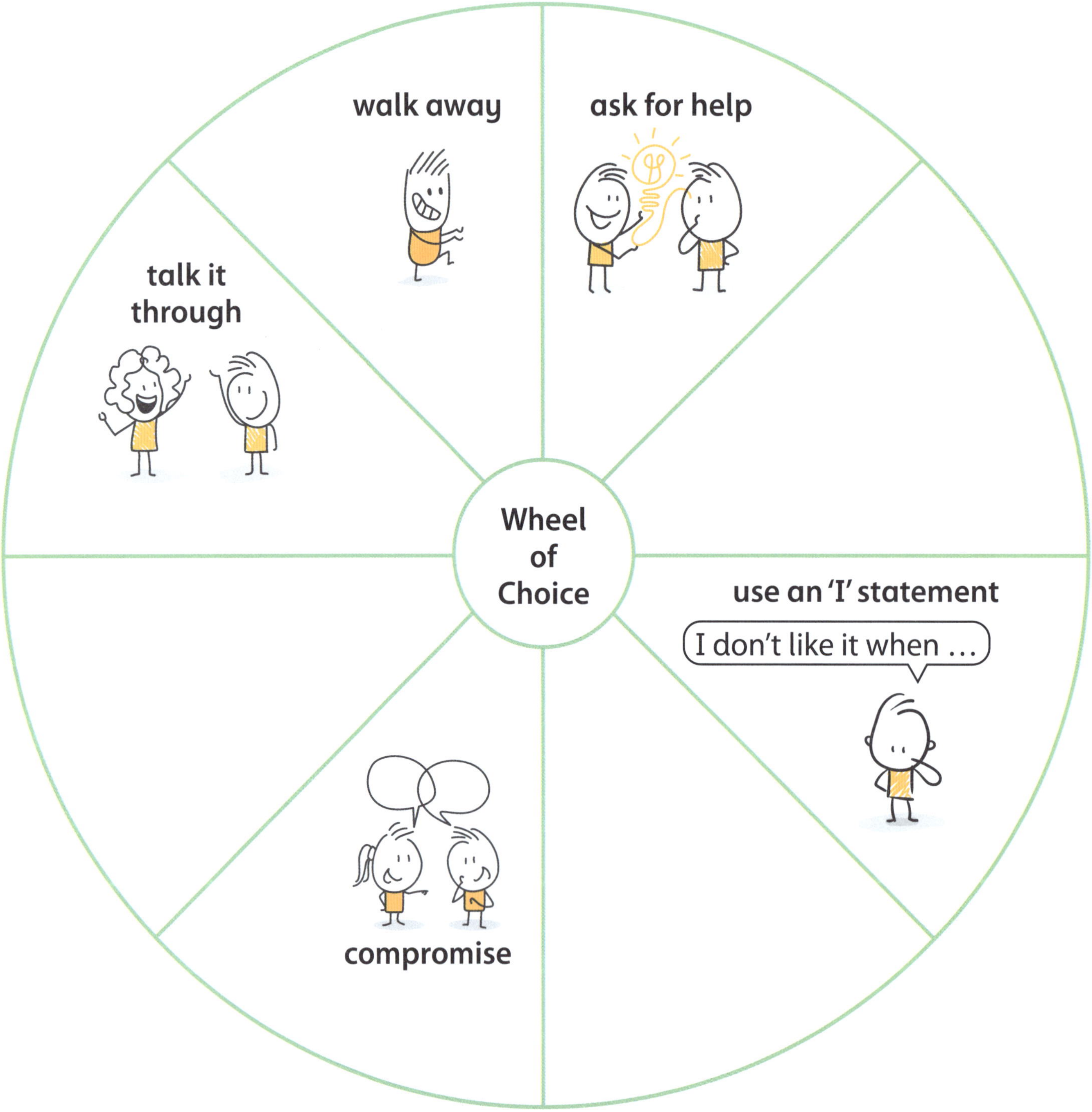

walk away

ask for help

talk it through

Wheel of Choice

use an 'I' statement

I don't like it when …

compromise

Compare your suggestions with a partner. What do you notice?

Look at this picture. What do you notice?

What might they think, believe or understand?

How might you help them to resolve (sort out) the conflict?

Share your thinking however you like. You could:

- act it out

- write it

- draw it ...

Being mindful means living in the now. We can be **balanced** and practise this by using our senses.

Look at this picture. What might you be able to hear, see, smell, taste or touch? Record your ideas around the picture.

Share your ideas with a partner.

How were your ideas similar or different?

What do you wonder about your partner's ideas?

Overcoming distractions

When we are distracted, we are unable to pay attention to something. We can learn how to deal with distractions.

When do you feel distracted?

How does being distracted make you feel?

Which learner profile attribute might help you to overcome distractions?

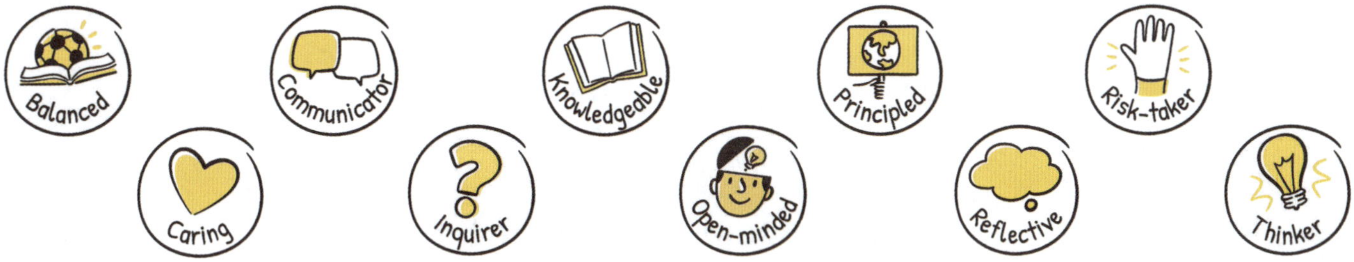

Balanced

Communicator

Knowledgeable

Principled

Risk-taker

Caring

Inquirer

Open-minded

Reflective

Thinker

Practising being present

Use your sense of hearing to connect to the present moment.

☐ Close your eyes for a minute and focus on what you can hear.

☐ Record the sounds that were closest to you in the smaller circle.

☐ Record the sounds that were further away in the bigger circle.

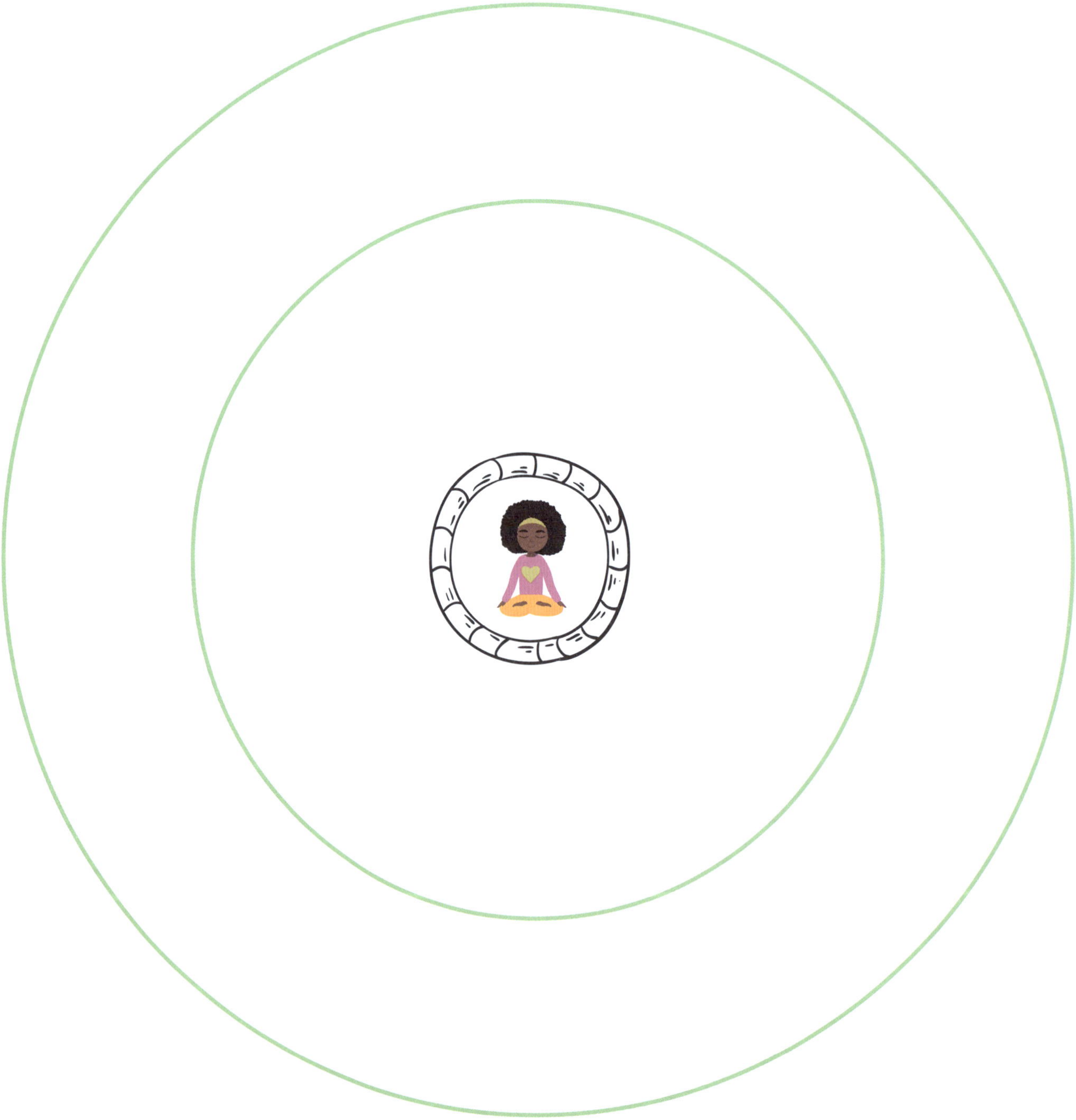

 How might using your senses help you to learn?

Using the senses

Sometimes, when we are distracted, it helps to bring ourselves back to the present.

Practice this strategy:

- stop what you are doing for a moment
- notice what you can see, hear and feel.

Things I can see

Things I can hear

Things I can feel

What are some ways you can manage distractions?

What tools and strategies can help you stay focused?

When I am distracted, I can …

Managing distractions will help me ....

....

....

The next time I get distracted, I will ....

....

Self-motivation

Self-motivation helps us to keep going and not give up. We can be **caring** and **balanced** by using **positive affirmations**. These help to motivate us.

What are some positive affirmations you can say to yourself?
For example: 'I am capable'.

self-motivation something inside that leads us to take action
positive affirmations kind things we say to ourselves

Using positive thinking

If you change your thoughts, you can change your mindset.
This will help you to become **balanced**.

- ☐ Think about a time when you have found something difficult.
- ☐ What were some negative thoughts you had?
- ☐ How could you have made your negative thoughts more positive?

☹	☺

Reflecting on my mindset

Think back to a learning experience from this past week that you found difficult.

Describe the learning experience.

What was difficult?

What thoughts did you have?
What was your self-talk?

What might you tell yourself next time you find something difficult?

Positive self-talk helps to keep us motivated, especially when things get difficult. It is a **balanced** and **caring** way of supporting yourself.

What could you say to yourself when you need help or motivation?
Draw yourself and add speech bubbles.

Keep going! You're doing great!

 Where could you keep these statements so you can see them when you need them?

Interpersonal relationships

Having strong relationships with people helps us develop attributes like being **caring**, a good **communicator** and **open-minded**.

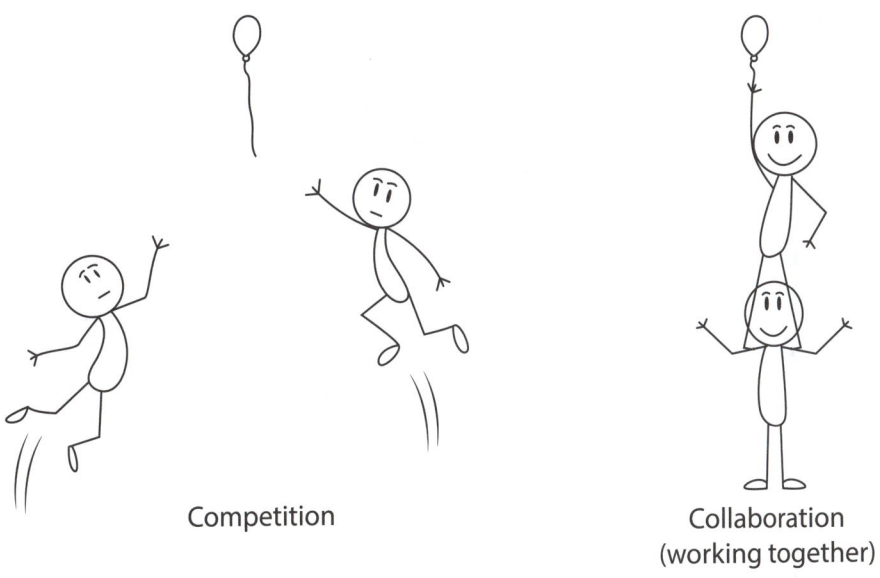

Competition

Collaboration
(working together)

How might these pictures help us to understand the importance of social skills and relationships?

Collaboration

Who did you collaborate with recently?

☐ Write their names and draw their faces.

☐ Write what they said in the speech bubbles.

....

How did collaboration support your learning? 😊

What did you not enjoy about collaborating? 🙁

 What have you learned about yourself through these collaborations?

How can you work well as a team?

☐ Complete the puzzle pieces to show your ideas. Try to fill them all in so you have a complete picture of what makes a great team!

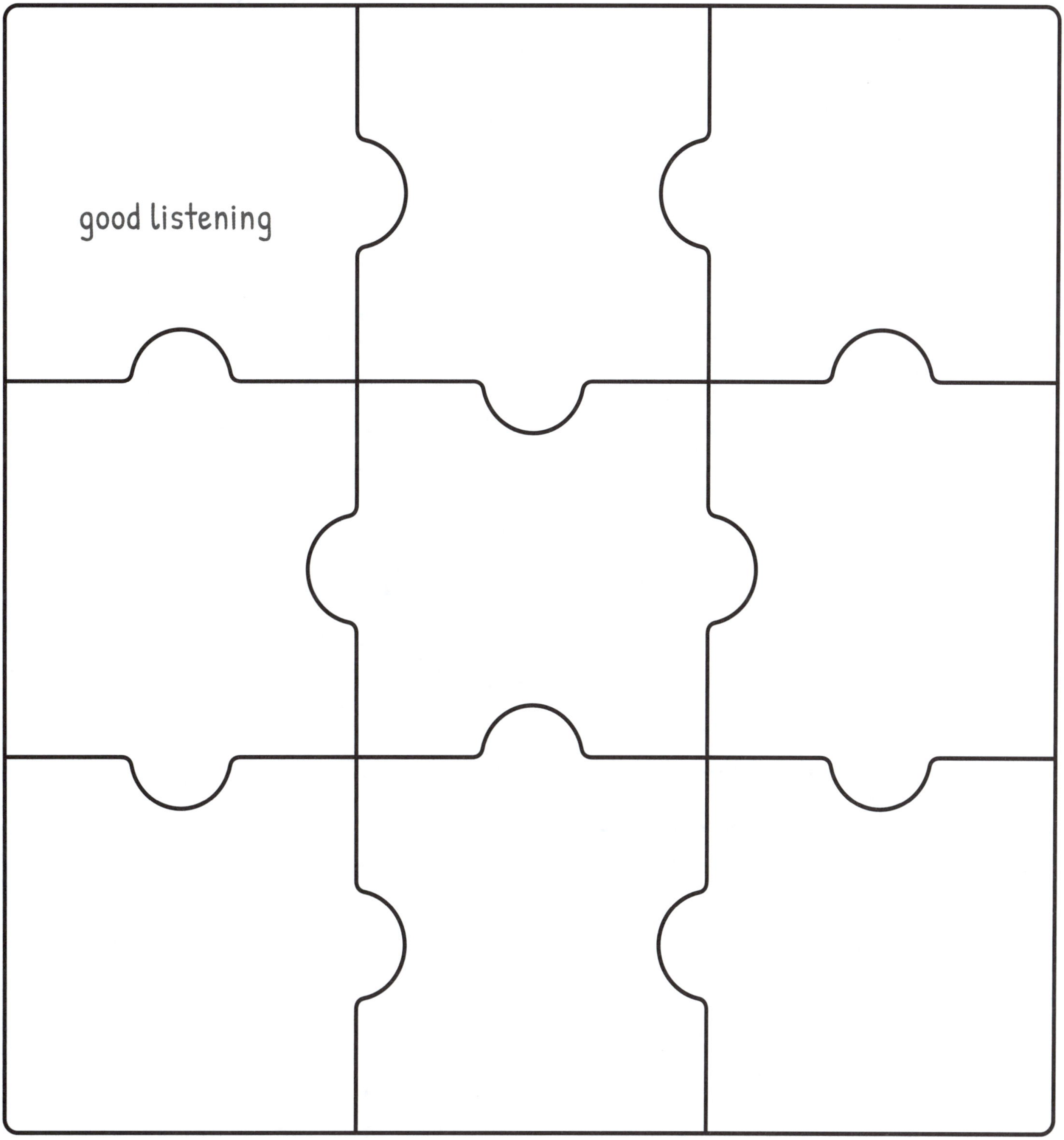

good listening

Taking action

A community project can involve two people or thousands! Community action means working as a team to share ideas, solve problems and bring change.

Think about your inquiry. How might community action make a difference? Record your ideas in the mind map.

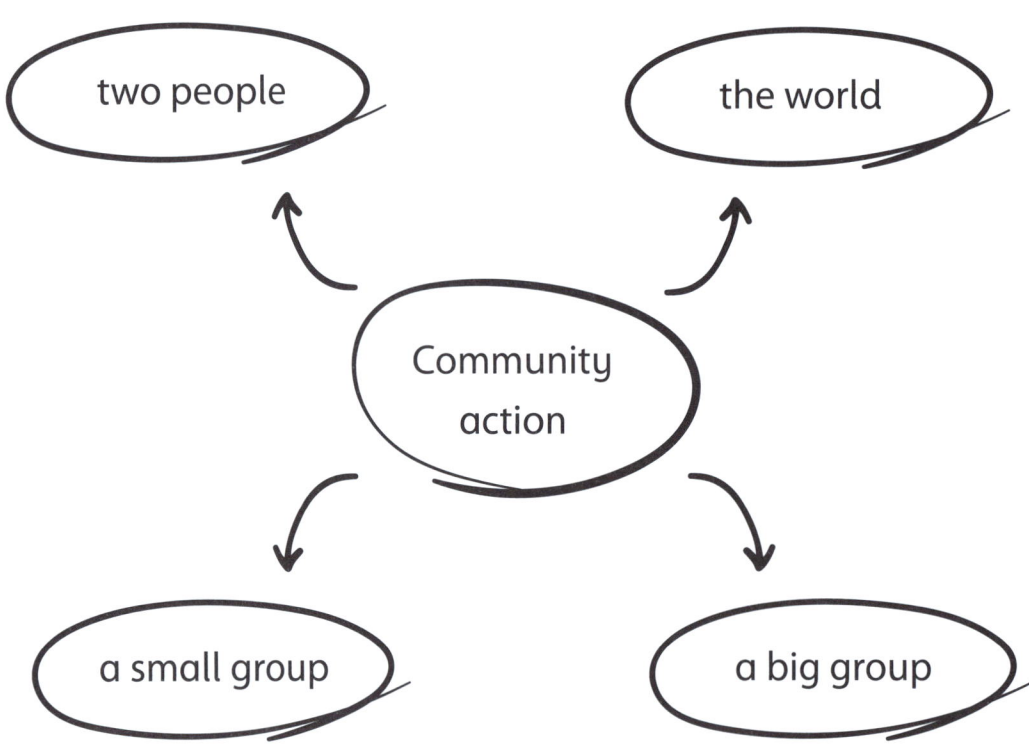

Exchanging information

We exchange information by talking, writing or using pictures. It helps us understand each other and learn new things.

How could you categorize these things?

cat   book   human   fish   frog   bread   owl   flower

Record your categories below.

 Discuss and compare your answers with a partner.

What is the same? What is different? Why might this be?

How have your learner profile attributes helped you to complete this activity?

Listening to others speak

> Listening to understand means giving our full attention to the speaker.
> Be **caring** and **open-minded** and try to understand their message.

☐ Share your categories from page 31 and explain your thinking.

☐ Listen carefully to your partner.

☐ Compare your thoughts in the table.

My thoughts	My partner's thoughts

How did your partner share their thoughts? What helped your understanding?

....

....

....

 How might listening to understand help you in the future?

How do you feel about speaking to an audience?

Record your thoughts in the chart below.

What do you **NEED** to know?

What **WORRIES** you about this?

What **EXCITES** you about this?

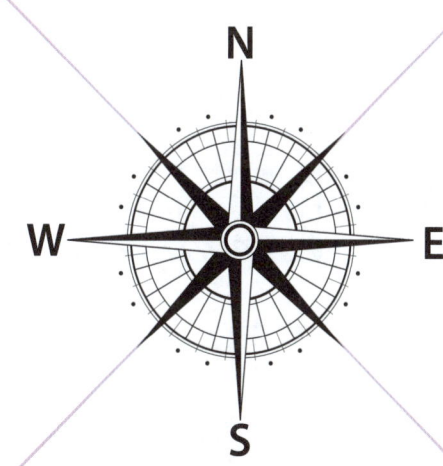

N

W — E

S

What might your next **STEPS** be?

What **SUGGESTIONS** could you make?

When we ask for help and support, we are being **risk-takers**.
It helps to be **open-minded** to other ideas and opinions.

☐ Reflect on your week.

☐ Colour in the things that are true for you and add your own.

This week I ...

helped someone

felt shy

shouted

created something new

broke a rule

felt worried

felt bullied

felt successful

hurt someone's feelings

made a mistake

I will share my ideas with: ....

Giving and receiving feedback

☐ Choose one of the finger puppet templates below.

☐ Put a piece of paper over the top and trace it or draw your own finger puppet.

☐ Cut it out. Stick the puppet together so it can go over your finger.

☐ Find another puppet to talk to.

☐ Tell the puppet what you have learned in your recent inquiry.

☐ Give the other puppet feedback on its communication skills.

 What feedback did you receive? How could it help you?

Taking action

A group of children decided to show how they were **caring**. Each child thought of one word that showed kindness. They created a banner of all of their words.

How could your communication skills be used to take action?

Ways of communicating

We use different types of communication to share our learning and present our thoughts and ideas to others.

☐ What types of communication have you used in the past?

☐ How did you use them?

How do you feel about trying new types of communication?

Trying different types of communication

Be a **risk-taker**.

☐ What types of communication are you comfortable using?

☐ What types of communication would you like to try? Add them to the toolbox.

  How can you be more of a **risk-taker**?

How could trying different types of communication support your learning?

How might regular feedback support you?

Planning how to communicate

Plan your presentation.

☐ Reflect on what you have been learning.

☐ How could you present what you have learned?

☐ What will you need?

What I KNOW	ACTION I will take	What I NEED

Taking action

Reflect on times when you've used these skills:

read for fun or to gather information

write about your thoughts and ideas

exchange information through listening and speaking

use technology to record or share information

How could you use these skills to help yourself?

....

....

....

....

How could you use these skills to help others?

....

....

....

....

Transferring knowledge

Being **knowledgeable** allows us to transfer our past knowledge to help us with new understanding.

knowledge strategies skills

transfer

My last inquiry

My new inquiry

Reflect on the graph below. What can you tell about this learner?

I am very knowledgeable

I don't have much knowledge

Insects	Well-being	Ecosystems	Energy

 Reflecting on what you already know can help you learn new things.
This person knows a lot about insects but very little about ecosystems.
Can any of their knowledge be transferred?

☐ What are you most/least knowledgeable about?

☐ Write an example in each yellow box.

☐ Reflect on where you are today with your knowledge.

☐ Colour the squares in the chart to show your self-assessment.

Five squares = lots of knowledge

One square = little knowledge

I am very knowledgeable about this

I don't have much knowledge about this

Things I am learning

Metacognition is thinking about our own thinking.
Being a **thinker** starts with understanding our own metacognition.

What other forms of thinking might you add to the raindrops?

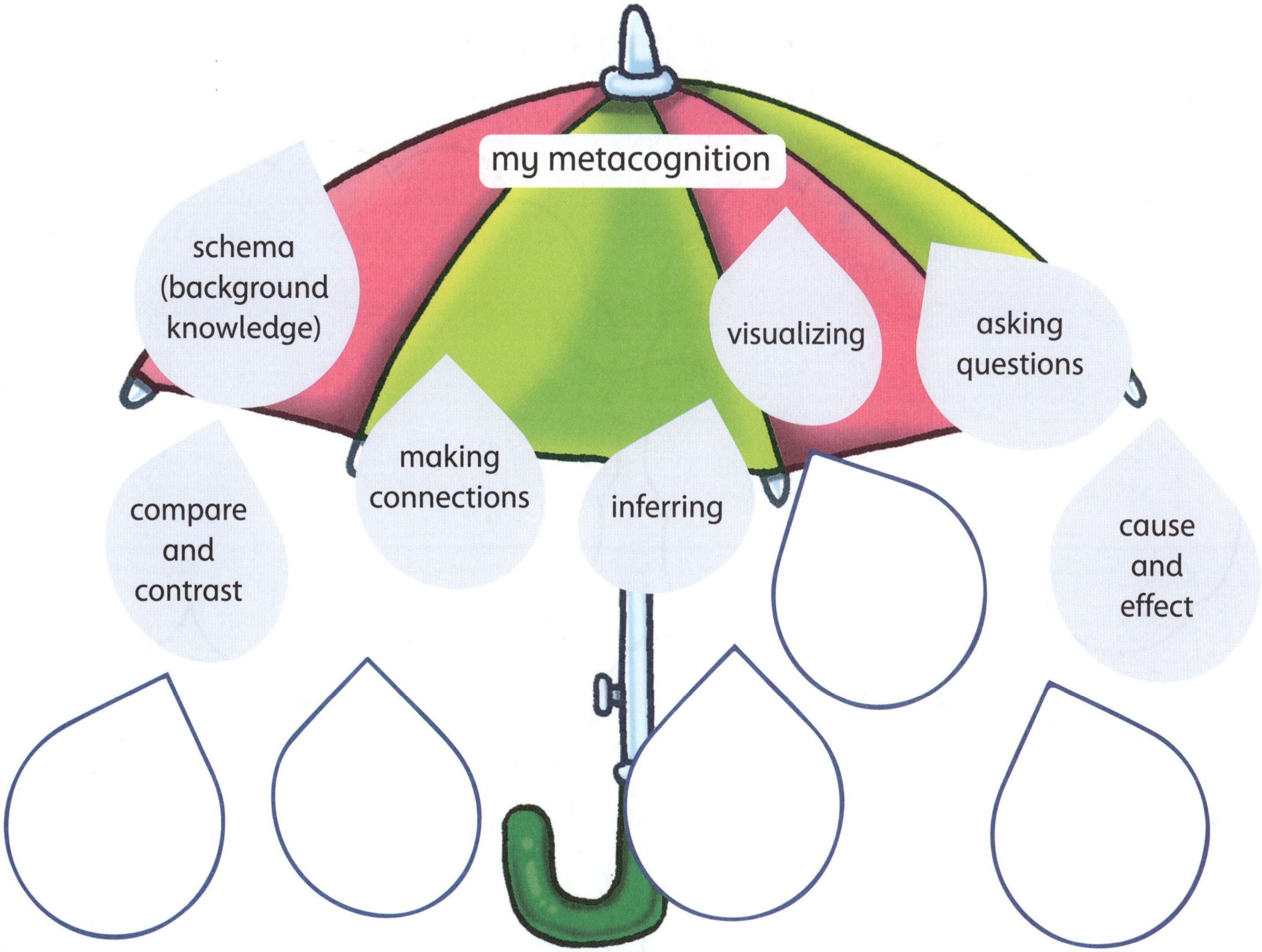

my metacognition

schema (background knowledge)

visualizing

asking questions

compare and contrast

making connections

inferring

cause and effect

Which type of thinking do you use most? How does it help you?
How could you improve your thinking skills by using metacognition?

Making connections

Making connections helps us to learn and understand things better. When we learn something new, we can think about how it's similar or different to things we've learned before.

What connections have you made within your unit of inquiry? Share your connections below.

 How has making connections helped your understanding?

Using metacognition to help my learning

Answer these questions about your metacognitive thinking.
Use page 43 to help you.

How has metacognitive thinking helped with your inquiry?

Which skills or strategies have you used?

Talk to a partner about how you used your metacognition recently.
Explain how it helped to support your learning.

Critical and creative thinking

Critical and creative thinking are your super powers!

I ask questions.

I look at things from different points of view.

critical thinker

I use my imagination to create new ideas.

I think of creative ways to solve problems.

creative thinker

When have you used ...

critical thinking?	creative thinking?

both critical and creative thinking?	What action did this lead to?

Thinking critically

Put these in order of speed, from fastest to slowest.

| car | bicycle | eagle | rowing boat | zebra |

Fastest

1 ....

2 ....

3 ....

4 ....

Slowest 5 ....

Compare your results with a partner. What do you notice?

47

Bee roads

Since the 1930s, England has lost over 90% of its flower meadows. This has caused problems for insects like bees and butterflies. Luckily, a charity is taking action!

Buglife is a charity in England. They have made a map of 'B-Lines'. These are places where they ask people to grow as many wild flowers as possible. Farmers and land owners are being asked to help – as well as people like you!

The idea is that these places will all join together to make insect 'roads'. Then bees and other insects can travel along them.

Bee roads are a creative way to solve a problem for wildlife and our environment.

How can you help bees and other pollinators?

Grow herbs or fruit

1 Reflect on the idea of a 'bee road' as a creative solution.

2 Discuss your reflection with a partner.

3 Apply your creative thinking skills.

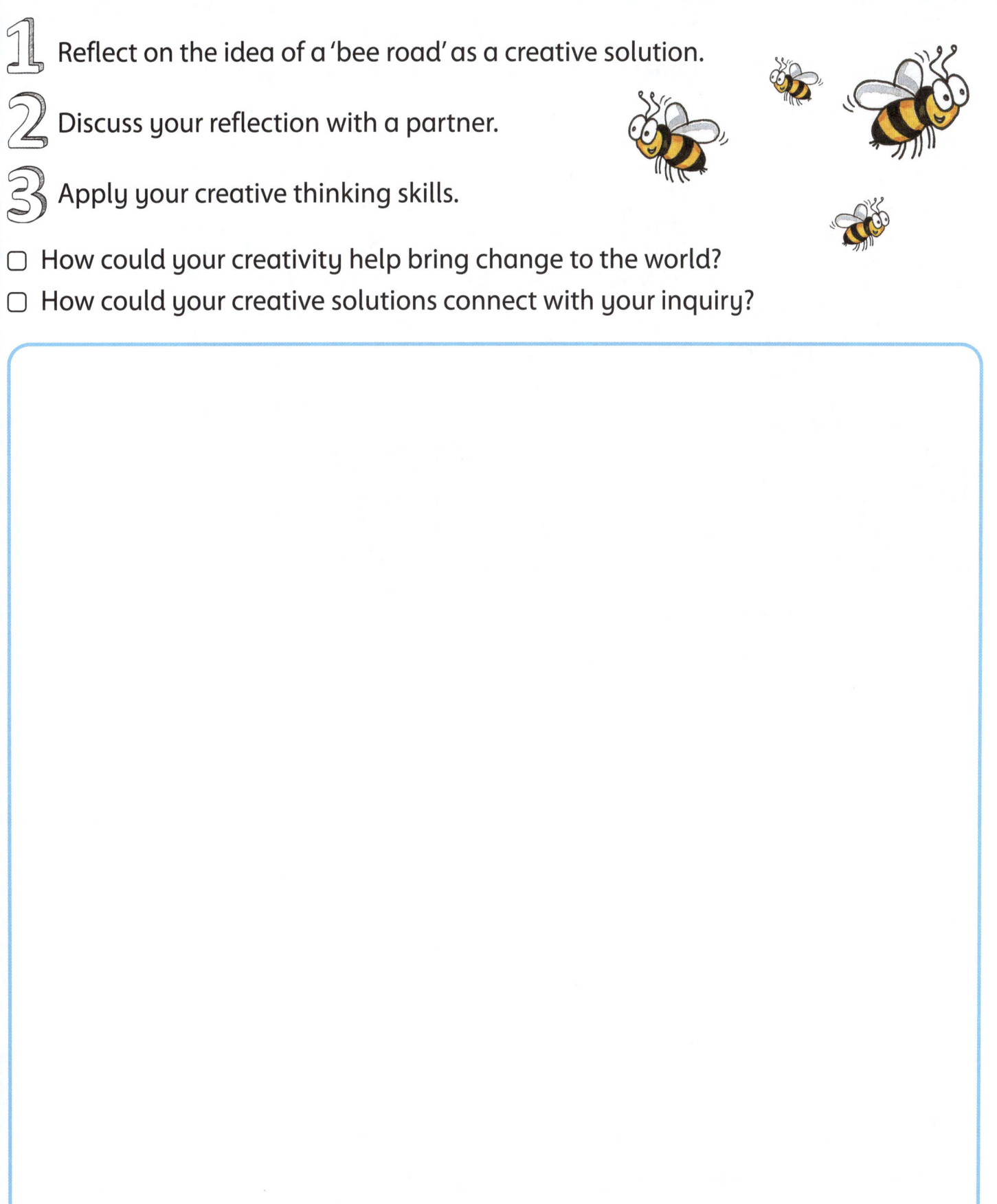

☐ How could your creativity help bring change to the world?

☐ How could your creative solutions connect with your inquiry?

Thinking and planning action

The Sustainable Development Goals are 17 goals that everyone in the world is working on together. The goals cover all areas of life.

 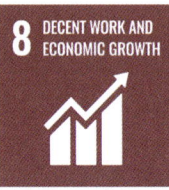    

How might these goals help guide our thinking?

 What local or global problems are you aware of?

What inspires you to take action from your unit of inquiry?

How do these problems connect with the United Nations SDGs?

When we see a problem in the world, we can be **thinkers** and come up with solutions. Thinking skills help us plan and organize our actions.

Plan to take action!

☐ Use your thinking skills to write an action plan.

☐ What materials will you need to create it?

☐ How might collaborating improve your plan?

 **Responsible consumption and production**
We must not waste resources
like food, water or energy.

 **Climate action**
We must take fast action
against the damage we are
doing to our planet.

 How might these goals connect?

Life below water

We must protect the oceans and
the animals that live in them.

Life on land

We must look after our land,
insects and animals.

 What if you had one goal to focus on?
How might that goal fit with your inquiry?

Choose one of these goals.

Why is this goal important?

What could the world look like if we achieve it?

What is taking action?

	What might action look like for myself and for others?
Personal action What personal action do I want to take?	
Community action What could I do for my local community?	
Global action How can I connect to the UN SDGs?	

Young people around the world have been **principled** and helped to create positive change.

Timoci Naulusala

In 2016, a cyclone (a spinning storm) hit Fiji. It caused huge damage to Timoci's village. The year after, when he was just 12 years old, Timoci spoke at a climate change conference in Germany. His speech was very powerful and helped to encourage action.

What do you wonder?

Thinking

Zach Bonner

After a hurricane (a big tropical storm) hit his town in Florida, Zach set to work helping people who were homeless.

He delivered 27 truckloads of water bottles to people in need when he was just six years old!

Leah Namugerwa

Leah lives in Uganda, where climate change has caused extreme weather. Sometimes there are droughts, where there is no rain. Other times there are floods. Leah has planted more than 3000 trees. These trees take up water when there is heavy rainfall. This helps to prevent floods.

 How might the learner profile connect with Zach and Leah's actions?

Who else do you know that has been **principled** and fought for what is right?
What did they do?

What do you
care about?

What do you
want to change?

People who make change are **principled**, but they are also **caring**, good **communicators**, **knowledgeable**, **risk-takers** and more!

Reflect on the quote.
Which attributes of your learner profile might help you to be the change?

"You must be the change you want to see in the world."

Gandhi

A **source** is a person, place or thing that we can get information from.

Write down as many sources of information as you can think of.

How many can you record?

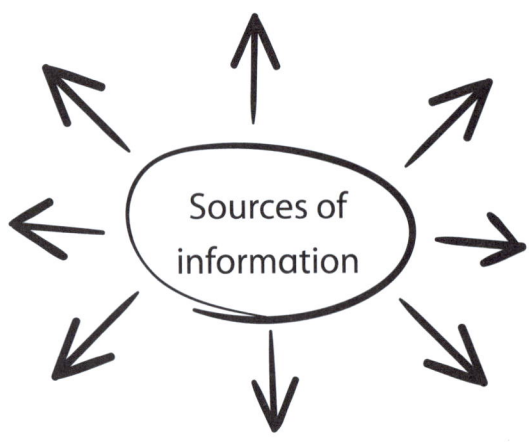

Sources of information

I thought of .... different sources of information.

Share your sources with your group.
How do your ideas compare?

Imagine you are researching an actor called Jordan Spark who has just starred in a new movie.

You want to learn about his background and his other movies.

Which website would you click on?

I would choose website ☐ because …

What information would you be looking for to learn about the actor's background?

....

....

Forming questions

What were your best questions in your inquiry?

What made those questions the best ones?

Using my thinking skills to develop an inquiry

Thinking, sharing and being curious helps us become great **inquirers**!

What do I want to know about this unit of inquiry?

What might I need to learn before I can investigate?

What skills will help me?

How has your metacognition helped your investigations?

Sources

- How did you search for information?
- What sources did you use?
- Which types of source did you find most/least useful? Why?

Presentation

- How did you show what you have learned?
- Did you enjoy using this type of communication?
- Was it easy to show others what you had learned?

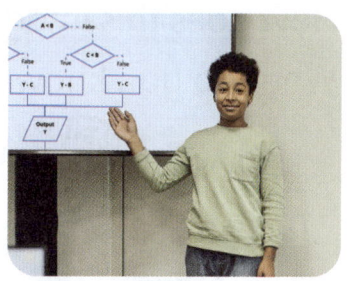

NURTURE
NATURE for the
FUTURE

 Discuss your thoughts and ideas with a partner.
- What do you notice?
- What might you change or try the next time?

Using media ethically

How does this image make you feel?

What do you know about ethical use of media?

> **ethical** what is best for yourself and society
>
> **media** ways of communicating like the internet, video games and television

I already know ...	I wonder ...

How confident do you feel about safety and responsibility when you are researching? Draw an arrow on the line.

I need a lot of help.   I feel comfortable, with some help.   I feel confident and independent.

Analyse the following webpage. Do you trust this information? Why or why not?

Add reasons and draw arrows to show which parts of the webpage you do not trust.

Be **principled**!

How can you use the internet responsibly? Write or draw your ideas below.

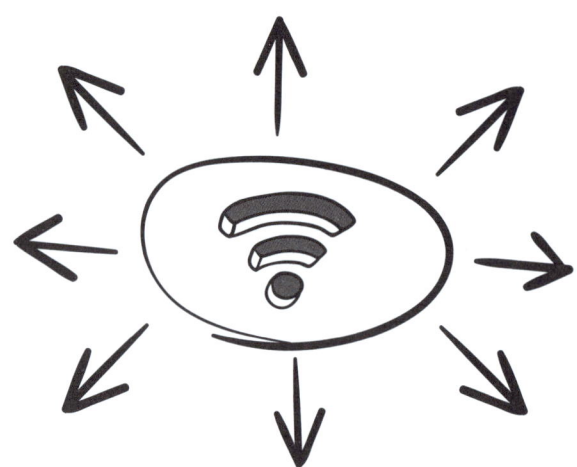

Taking action

Reflect on your unit of inquiry. Who might benefit from your action?
Write or draw some ideas below.

The natural world 	Local community 
People around the world 	Me! 

 What connections can you make with the Sustainable Development Goals?

Reflecting on my year

Something I learned ...

Something I am proud of ...

The SDG I thought about the most was ...

The learner profile attribute that I used the most was ..

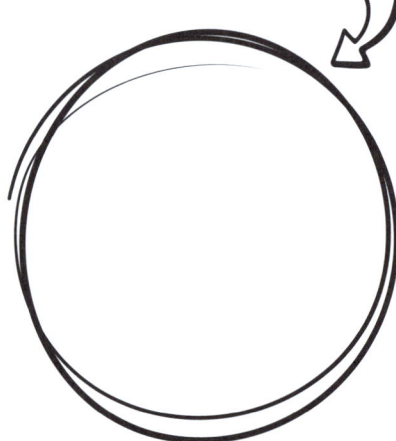

The book I loved the most was about …

....

....

....

....

A memory I'll keep …

....

....

....

This is a drawing of …

....

....

....

....

What's next?

What are your hopes for next year?